"Pray without
Ceasing."
1 Thessalonians 5 : 17

A Prayer Guide and Journal

by

Ruth Hampton

Copyright

Copyright © [2025] by [Ruth Hampton Writes, LLC]

All rights reserved.

No part of this publication may be reproduced, distributed, or transmitted in any form or by any means, including photocopying, recording, or other electronic or mechanical methods, without the prior written permission of the publisher, except as permitted by U.S. copyright law.

This book is dedicated to "Our Father", who art in Heaven *(Matthew 6:9)*. The one who allowed me to write this book to encourage others to serve Jesus Christ.

To my children (Joshua and Jasmyne) and grandchildren (Alayziah, Ma'Kiyah, Lorenzo, and Lamarco). The ones who motivate me to keep striving for success.

To my parents (Elijah Hampton, Sr. and Mae Covington-Hampton for birthing me and teaching me about Christ Jesus.

To my paternal and maternal grandmothers (Zera Amerson-Hampton and Annie Mae Robinson- Covington--both deceased). The anointed ones who started the foundation of Christ and instilled the love of God in my parents' hearts. This led to my parents' *salvation and accepting Christ in their lives!*

To my siblings and umpteen nieces and nephews (lol). They keep me filled with laughter and love.

Finally, I dedicate this book to everyone who purchases it and truly reads it:) Be inspired; be empowered. **"God is Calling...Please Answer***!"* Be blessed!

Introduction

God is calling us for so many reasons. HE is Omniscient (all knowing), Omnipresent (everywhere at one time), and Omnipotent (all powerful). He wants us to know that the harvest is great but the laborers are few; so pray earnestly that God will send forth laborers into His harvest (**Matthew 9:37-38**).

Just like Uncle Sam is looking for those to join the military, God is seeking servants- laborers- to work for HIM. He tells us in His Word to "deny yourself, take up your cross, and follow me (**Matthew 16:24**)."

You are probably thinking to yourself: "What can I do for *HIM*?;" "How can *HE* use me?;" "Why would *HE* want me?;" "What is *HE* calling me to do?"

This is where you should do some "soul searching" to evaluate or re-evaluate your personal relationship with God. As Christians and believers of Jesus Christ, we are suppose to "study to show ourselves approved" (2 Timothy 2:15). Ask God for knowledge, wisdom, and understanding (Proverbs 2:1-11).

The basis for this prayer guide and journal are as follows:
- to introduce or to reconnect you with God; **or**
- to start, continue, or resurrect your prayer life; **or**
- to help you find your purpose in what God wants you to do.

You may use the journal to record your prayers, thoughts, and notes if you desire to do so. Remember God loves you (John 3:16). Will you answer God's call today?

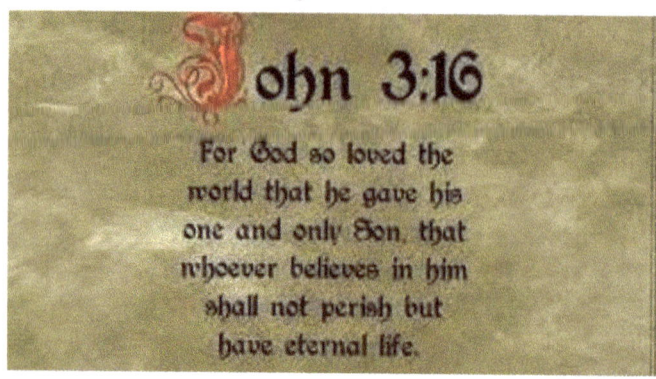

John 3:16
For God so loved the world that he gave his one and only Son, that whoever believes in him shall not perish but have eternal life.

Prayer Industries, Inc.

Mobile: +A LLW-IRE-LESS   **email:** pray2God@anytime.hvn
ADDRESS: 365 Daily Prayer St.
Heav, EN 12667

MEMORANDUM

To: Everyone

From: God The Father, The Son, and The Holy Spirit

Date: AL/WA/YS

Re: Daily Prayer

Watch therefore, and pray always, that you may be accounted worthy to escape all these things that shall come to pass, and stand before ME (**Luke 21:36**). Watch and pray that you may not enter into temptation (**Matthew 26:41**).
You ought to pray always and not faint (**Luke 18:1**). "I AM" in need of faithful hearers and doers of God's Word (**James 1:22-25**).
If you have any questions, then please feel free to reach ME (Jesus Christ) through prayer, and I will respond (**Matthew 7:8**).
Thank you for your prompt attention in this matter.

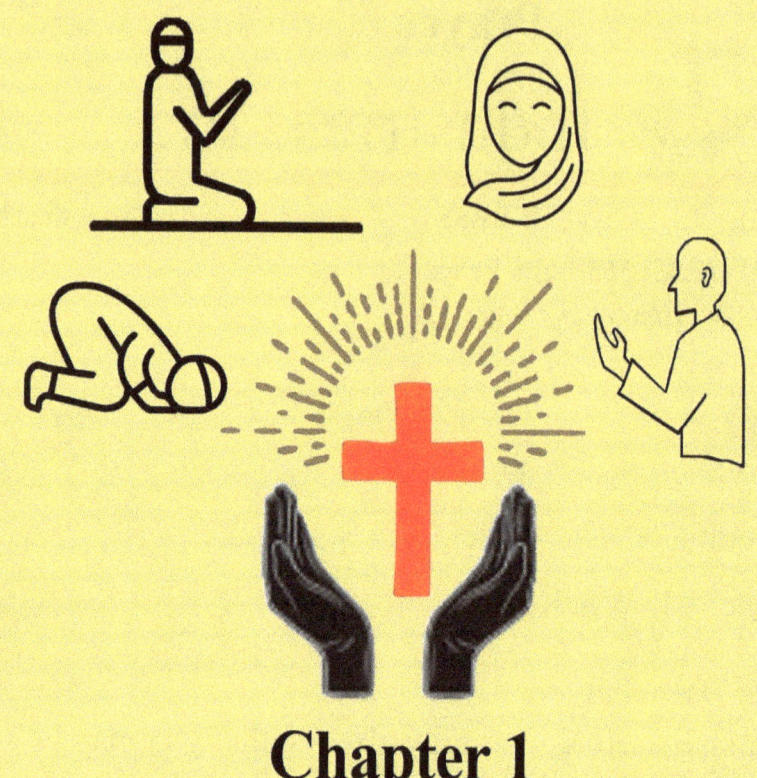

Chapter 1

God Is Calling
For
Prayer Warriors

Prayer

The Lord's Prayer

Matthew 6:9-13

Our Father which art in heaven, Hallowed be thy name.

Thy kingdom come. Thy will be done in earth, as it is in heaven.

Give us this day our daily bread.

And forgive us our debts, as we forgive our debtors.

And lead us not into temptation, but deliver us from evil: For thine is the kingdom, and the power, and the glory, forever. Amen

Prayer

The Serenity Prayer

God grant me the Serenity to accept the things I cannot change, the Courage to change the things I can, and the Wisdom to know the difference.

W ho should pray?

Everyone should pray..."But as for me, my prayer is unto thee, O LORD, in an acceptable time: O God, in the multitude of thy mercy hear me, in the truth of thy salvation" (**Psalm 69:13**). "If my people who are called by my name, will humble themselves and pray and seek my face and turn from their wicked ways, then I will hear from heaven, and I will forgive their sin and will heal their land" (**2 Chronicles 7: 14**).

Don't allow anyone to tell you that God will not hear you. There are plenty of times when I was a sinner, I called on the name of the Lord, and He answered me (sometimes speedily). Well, you are certainly not going to call on the devil to help you! Are you? Satan is the reason you need to call on the name of the LORD! You may not always like the answer, but HE will respond. Jesus is ready and willing to save your soul no matter what you have done or are doing wrong. Remember, HIS hand is not so short that it cannot save (**Isaiah 59:1**).

What is prayer?

Prayer is direct communication with God. You are talking to Him at first hand...**Philippians 4:6** "Be careful for nothing; but in everything by prayer and supplication with thanksgiving let your requests be made known unto God."

Prayer, according to **Merriam-Webster**, is defined as: (1) an act or practice of praying to God or a god; (2) an earnest request or wish.

When should you pray?

You can pray to God daily at anytime.
- **1 Thessalonians 4:17** "Pray continually..."
- **Daniel 6:10** "Now when Daniel knew that the writing was signed, he went into his house...kneeled upon his knees three (3) times a day, and prayed and gave thanks before his God..."
- **Psalms 55:17** "Evening, and morning, and at noon, will I pray, and cry aloud: and HE (God) shall hear my voice."

Prayer

Where can you pray?

You can pray to God anywhere (e.g., home, church, school, hospital, prison/jail, job, etc.,). God is omnipresent! He is everywhere! "The eyes of the LORD are in every place, beholding the evil and the good." **Proverbs 15:3**

Why should you pray?

You should pray to show your gratitude (thankfulness) toward our Creator (GOD). "Give thanks to the Lord, for HE is good and HIS mercy endures forever." **1Chronicles 16:34**

You should pray to repent of your sins. "HE is the atoning sacrifice for our sins, and not only for ours, but also for the sins of the whole world." **1 John 2:2**

Confess your sins to God and HE will deliver you. "If you declare with your mouth, 'Jesus is Lord' and believe in your heart that God hath raised him (Jesus) from the dead, you will be saved." **Romans 10:9**

You should pray to forgive, not only others, but also, ourselves. "For if you forgive other people when they sin against you, your heavenly Father will also forgive you." **Matthew 6:14**

How should you pray?

You can pray **standing** (as Solomon did) "he stood before the alter of the Lord in the presence of all the congregation of Israel, and spread forth his hands:" **2 Chronicles 6:12**

You can pray **kneeling** (as Daniel did) "....he kneeled upon his knees three (3) times a day, and prayed..." **Daniel 6:10**
When HE (Jesus) withdrew about a stone's throw beyond them, HE knelt down and prayed, **Luke 22:41**

You can pray **sitting** (as David did) "Then went king David in, and sat before the LORD..," **2 Samuel 7:18**

You can pray with your **face to the ground-prostate position-**(as Jesus did in the Garden of Gethsemane) "and HE went a little further and fell on HIS face, and prayed..." **Matthew 26:39**

You can pray **lying down** to meditate on HIM..."Tremble and do not sin; when you are on your beds, search your hearts and be silent" **Psalms 4:4**. "On my bed I remember you; I think of you through the watches of the night" **Psalms 63:6**.

You should learn how to pray "in Jesus' name" **John 16:23-24**.

In Jesus' Name

I remember in my youthful days hearing various Pastors and ministers say "Just ask in Jesus' name and you will receive (**Matthew 21:22**)." Well, there were a lot of toys I didn't receive (LOL). As I grew older, I didn't get that ideal marital relationship either-twice (LOL).

Instead of "mapping out" my prayers about what I need or my "heart's desires." I just say a lot of words and end the prayer with *"In Jesus' Name."* Not realizing that my wants or "heart's desires" may not be in God's plans for me. For example, it is my heart's desire to have a Can-Am bike (3-wheel motorcycle). I don't know that God feels I should have that. Even though scripture says that "God will give you the desires of your heart" if you delight yourself in Him (**Psalm37:4**). There's always an obstacle every time I try to get that Can-Am. God is Omniscient (all-knowing)! Maybe HE is shielding me from an unforeseen accident. Who knows? I sure don't question it anymore!

In Jesus' Name

If you can consult physicians, lawyers, or auto mechanics about your concerns, maybe you should "map out" your prayers before praying. Are we afraid HE may not agree with our prayer; or even hear it? What about our state of mind when we pray? Are we focused or confused? Are we covetous when we pray? Below is an example of a prayer "double bubble map." Why do you need or want what you're praying for? Try it out; or not.

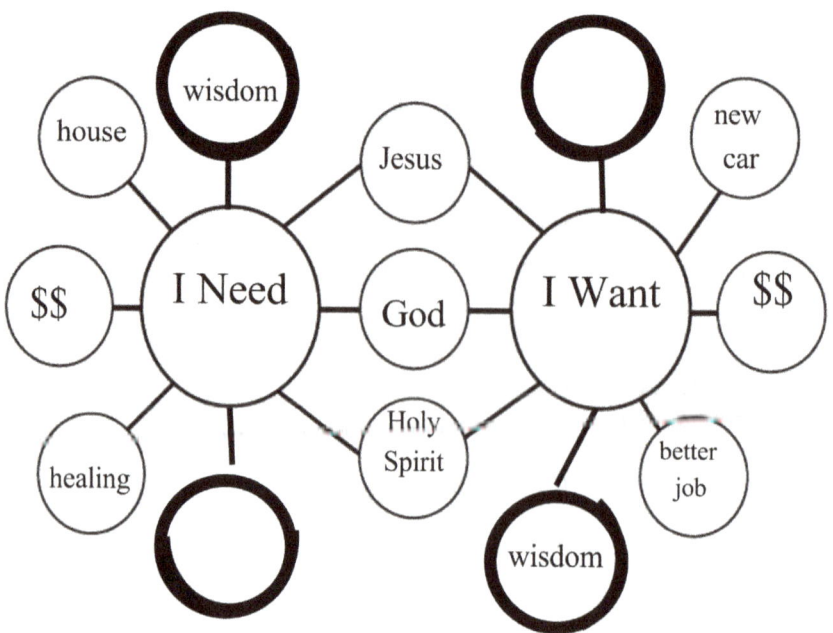

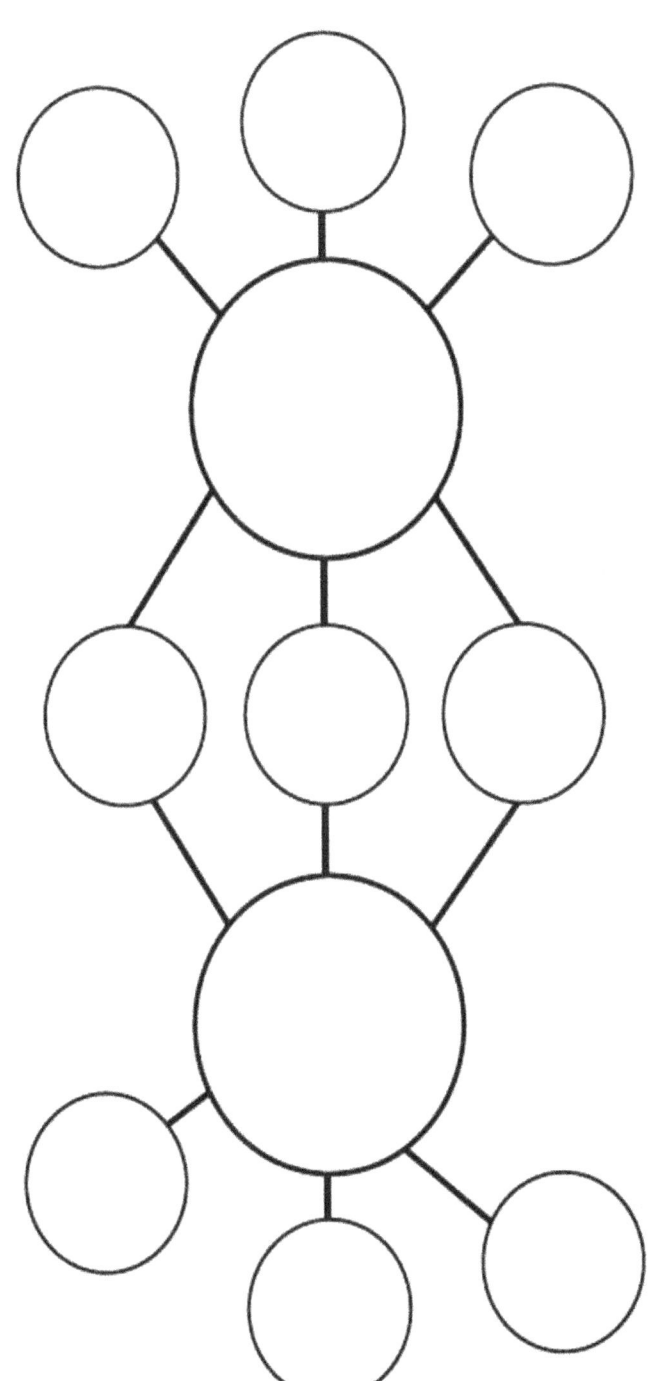

Prayer

In Jesus' Name

I wonder if some of my prayers are/were delayed or denied because of my "much speaking" or "asking amiss" or "unknowingly praying out of God's will."

The Bible declares that when you pray, do not keep on babbling or using vain repetitions or jargon like heathens and hypocrites do. They think they will be heard because of their many words (**Matthew 6:7**); *"much speaking."*

When you ask "in Jesus' name," maybe you do not receive, because you ask with the wrong motives, (**James 4:3**) or you're trying to keep up with the Joneses-*"asking amiss."*

The Spirit of the Lord helps you with your prayers. When you do not know what you ought to pray for, the Spirit himself intercedes for you through wordless groans. And HE who searches our hearts knows the mind of the Spirit, because the Spirit intercedes for God's people in accordance with the will of God

Prayer

In Jesus' Name

(**Romans 8:26-27**)-"*unknowingly praying out of God's will.*" Anything we pray for, we should ask according to God's will, He hears us" (**1 John 5:14**).

Friends, when you pray to God, just talk to him in a "normal," "down-to-earth" tone. Be yourself. You don't have to be pretentious with God. That's what I love about Him! God even has a sense of humor! Open up to Him, and you will see what I mean:)

I am a little mature in Christ now; therefore, I end all my prayers on this note:

"Dear Lord,
I pray

_____

Thank you Lord in advance for answering this prayer.
I pray this is the right
prayer. If not, then please intercede on my behalf.
Teach me how to pray,
oh God. In Jesus' name. Amen."

Prayer

Who is Jesus to to you?

Jesus is a *miracle worker* (Psalms 77:14).

Jesus is a *wonderful counselor* (Isaiah 9:6).

Jesus is a *healer* (Exodus 15:26).

Jesus is a *provider* (Philippians 4:19).

Jesus is a *protector* (Psalms 91).

Jesus is a *deliverer from sin* (1 John 5:4-5).

Prayer

Jesus is the "bread of life." **John 6:35**-"And Jesus said unto them, I am the bread of life; he that cometh to me shall never hunger; and he that believeth on me shall never thirst." **John 6:33**-"For the bread of God is HE which cometh down from Heaven and giveth light unto the world."

Jesus is a disciplinarian. **Hebrews 12:5-6**-"My son/daughter do not regard lightly the discipline of the Lord, nor be weary when reproved by Him. For the Lord disciplines (chastises) the ones HE loves, and chastises (disciplines) every son/daughter whom HE receives."

Who or What is Jesus to you?
Write in the empty space below..

My prayer today is

Chapter 2

God Is Calling For Praisers and Worshippers

"Let everything that hath breath praise the Lord. Praise ye the Lord." (Psalms 150:6)

# My Song of Praise

Worship is a form of divine devotion and extreme loyalty to something or someone. Some people worship material things, idols, other gods, or each other. God wants us to be true to HIM; serve HIM only (**1 Corinthians 8:6**).

When I close my eyes during worship and think on all the wondrous miracles God has done in my life, I can't help but shed tears of joy. Protect your worship and praise. The enemy (the devil) comes to steal, kill, and destroy (**John 10:10**).

My worship to God signifies how dedicated and committed I am to serving HIM. My worship to God teaches me not to be ashamed of my Father who art in Heaven (**Matthew 6:9**). My worship to God allows me to sing HIS praises in the midst of my storms (**Ephesians 5:19**). My worship to God brings me faith, wisdom, joy, and peace.

Will you put away your idols and other gods and worship the LORD today?

My Song of Praise

Praise and worship allows us to acknowledge and feel God's presence in our sanctuary (**Psalms 150:1**). A sanctuary is a safe place of refuge or protection; a consecrated place. Whether it's at church, home, or prayer closet, etc. We don't have to wait until we get to church to praise and worship God.

Praise and worship is a sacrificial offering to the Lord (**Hebrews 13:15**). It does not matter how tired or discouraged we may feel; we should still praise God because of his mighty works and many blessings (**John 3:16; Romans 11:36; Isaiah 25:1; Psalms 24:1-10**).

There are many ways to praise and worship God. You can sing, dance, shout, clap your hands, stomp your feet, play musical instruments. You can even sway back and forth! Just praise and worship Him in your own way; it is pleasing in His sight!

But the hour cometh, and now is, when the true worshippers shall worship the Father in spirit and in truth: for the Father seeketh such to worship him (John 4:23-24).

# My Song of Praise

Praise the Lord. Praise Jesus for the miraculous works HE is doing, has done, and will do in my life. **(Luke 1:37)**

Praise the Lord for helping me when I did not think I could make it by myself. **(Isaiah 41:10)**

Praise the Lord for reassuring me constantly that "I will never leave you, nor forsake you." **(Deuteronomy 31:8)**

Praise the Lord for HIS protection and mercy as I travel near and far. **(Proverbs 18:10)**

Praise the Lord for grace when I strayed from HIM and my Christian journey. **(Isaiah 53:6)**

# My Song of Praise

Praise the Lord for HIS patience. **(2 Peter 1:6)**

Praise the Lord for exposing my spiritual gifts and natural talents to me (and how to use them for HIS glory). **(James 1:17)**

Praise the Lord for being a forgiving, understanding, and merciful God. **(Psalms 86:5)**.

Praise the Lord for showing me the error of my ways. **(Hebrews 12:5-6)**

Praise the Lord for HIS compassion when I was disobedient and rebellious to HIS will; afraid to go HIS way. **(Psalms 51:1)**

My Song of Praise

Praise God in the sanctuary (**Psalms 150:1**).

Praise God for singing, music, and dance (**Psalms 149:1-3**).

Praise God for hymns and spiritual songs (**Colossians 3:16**); (**Ephesians 5:19**).

Praise God for worship (**John 4:23-24**); (**Luke 4:8**); (**Psalms 29:2**); (**Psalms 95:6**).

What is your song of praise?

"Every day will I bless thee; and I will praise thy name forever and ever." (**Psalms 145:2**)

My prayer today is

Chapter 3

**God Is Calling
For
Souls to
Surrender**

Surrender

What does it mean to "surrender?" Well, it simply means to give yourself up completely. Some people feel that "surrender" means to accept defeat. One might think of **war**-giving oneself up to the enemy; so, he/she feels they have to fight-never give up; never surrender. My **war**; my battle.

The fight is against **sin**. The **enemy** is Satan, the devil, the adversary (**1 Peter 5:8, Job 1:12, Luke 4:1-2**).
I used to hear the elders say, "old slew foot." What is *sin*? Sin is the transgression (trespasses) against the laws of God-when one knowingly goes against God's commandments.

From our youth many of us are taught about the obvious sins-the outer man (e.g., alcoholism, drugs, murder, adultery, pride, hatred, idolatry, lying, jealousy, etc.); while the hidden sins-the inner man (e.g., pride, covetousness, jealousy, envy, grudges, evil thoughts, lusts, etc.) are not taught in depth because they're internal. Nonetheless, God sees the works of the outer and inner man.

Ask God to reveal to you your sins. Ask Him to

Surrender

forgive you of your sins; and create within you a clean heart **(Psalms 51:10-13)**. Repent (surrender from sin), and acknowledge, and confess your sins unto God **(Romans 10:9-11; 1 John 1:9; Acts 2:38; Psalms 32:5)**. If there is anything within you that does not condemn you, then neither will HE-it's between you and God (**1 John 3:21**). It is not our place to judge nor condemn anyone (**Matthew 7:1-5**).

Surrendering *from sin* and surrendering *to God* are two separate actions. In order to do this, one must submit him-/herself to God (surrender to God); resist the devil (surrender from sin), and he (Satan) will flee **(James 4:7)**.

Surrender

Are we an **imperfect** people that "we have not all sinned and fallen short of the glory of God **(Romans 3:23)**? **Yes**. "If we say that we have no sin, we deceive ourselves, and the truth is not in us." **(1 John 1:8)**. Christians and believers of Jesus Christ, let's not get it "twisted;" feeling that it is okay to commit sin on a whim or at the drop of a hat; for we are all without excuse **(Romans 1:20)**.

Yes, God will forgive you of your sins if you confess with your mouth **(1 John 1:9)**; however, the Word of God declares that when one "willfully or deliberately" sins consistently (after coming into the knowledge of the truth), there is no more sacrifice of sins **(Hebrews 10:26)**. It is fearful to fall into the hands of the living God **(Hebrews 10:31)**.

Surrender

The law is commonly correlated to the "Ten Commandments" which were given to Moses on Mount Sinai after leading the people out of Egypt **(Exodus 20:1- 17)**. God wants us to repent (change from sinner to serve HIM) and keep HIS commandments **(Matthew 22:37-9; 1 John 3:4-6; Romans 7:7; John 1:17)**.

Surrender to God today for He is faithful and will not allow us to be tempted above our ability, (but with the temptation), He will provide a way of "escape" that we will be able to bear it **(1 Corinthians 10:13)**. Acknowledge that He is Lord, trust and believe in Him, and serve Him only (**Proverbs 3: 5-6**); (**Deuteronomy 13:4**); (**John 12:26**); (**Philippians 2:10-11**). Believe. Repent. Be Baptized (**Acts 2:38**).

When God opened my eyes about sin and the errors of my ways, I can't bring myself to deliberately go against His Word. Do I willfully sin? **No**. Do I make mistakes? **Yes**. Am I perfect? **I think not**. Nevertheless, I do **surrender from sin**; for the wages of sin is death **(Romans 6:23)**. I do **surrender to God**; for the gift of God is eternal life (**John 10:28**).

~Surrender~

Won't you surrender to God today?

Award-winning gospel singer, *Tamela Mann's*, verse of "Take Me To the King" states:

*"Take me to the King
I don't have much to bring.
My heart is torn in pieces. Here's my offering...
I surrender all!"*

(I do NOT own the copyrights to this song; neither is this solicitation to purchase the artist's music. I do NOT receive any compensation from the artist for mentioning this song.)

My prayer today is

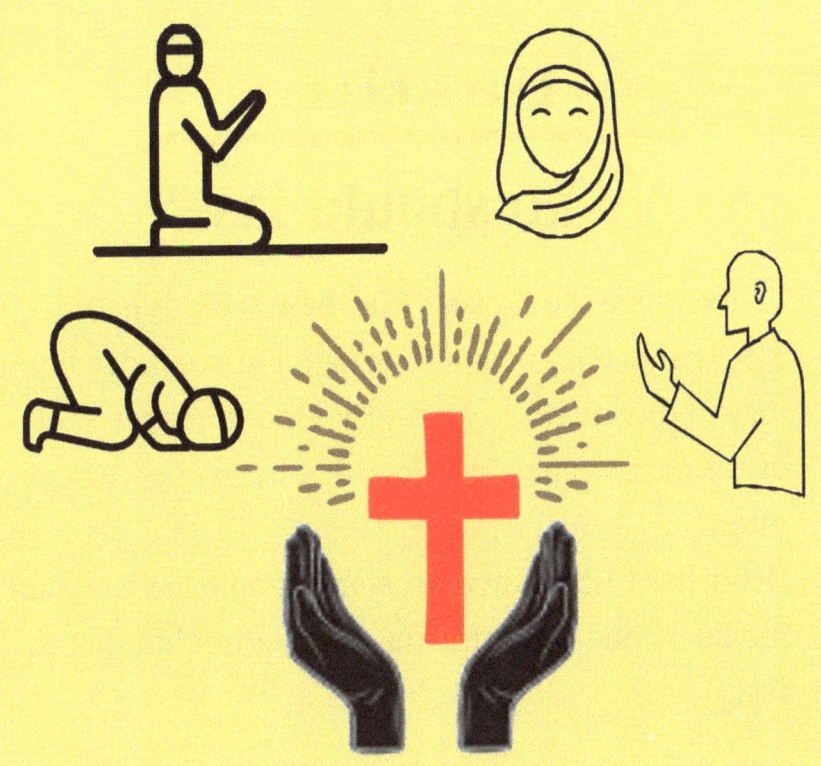

Chapter 4

God Is Calling For US to Fast

Disclaimer: Please consult your medical doctor before participating in any type of fast.

Fasting

Who should fast?

Everyone should fast (**Matthew 9:15; Jonah 3:5-9**) at his/her own discretion. I'm not judge nor jury in this matter. You seek God in prayer. Let every man/woman be persuaded by his/her own mind
(Romans 14:5); however, some people have certain medical conditions that may not permit him/her to fast.

It is encouraged to consult your medical doctor before partaking in any type of fast.

What is fasting?

The religious term, *"fasting,"* is to sacrificially abstain or refrain from eating food or drink so that you can focus solely on communicating with God. Fasting should be one's own preference based on his/her personal relationship with God. There are different types of fasts. The three (3) familiar fasts are:

Fasting

Who should fast?

Everyone should fast (**Matthew 9:15; Jonah 3:5-9**) at his/her own discretion. I'm not judge nor jury in this matter. You seek God in prayer. Let every man/woman be persuaded by his/her own mind
(Romans 14:5); however, some people have certain medical conditions that may not permit him/her to fast.

It is encouraged to consult your medical doctor before partaking in any type of fast.

What is fasting?

The religious term, *"fasting,"* is to sacrificially abstain or refrain from eating food or drink so that you can focus solely on communicating with God. Fasting should be one's own preference based on his/her personal relationship with God. There are different types of fasts. The three (3) familiar fasts are:

Fasting

- **N****ormal fast**-no food but able to drink juice/water (**Matthew 4:1-4**)
- **Daniel/partial fast**-giving up a certain food and/or drink (meats, desserts, coffee, wine, etc.) or skipping a meal (**Daniel 1:12; 10:3**)
- **Absolute fast**-no eating and no drinking (**Exodus 34:28; Deuteronomy 9:9; 9:18; Acts 9:9**).

When should you fast?

Fasting is a choice and at your own discretion. *It is important to talk to your medical doctor first before participating in a fast.*

When you fast depends on the type of fast you choose. I find it's best to consult God through prayer as to when HE would prefer you fast and for whatever the reason may be.

I do the absolute fast (morning for 1-4 hours) without food or drink. Also, I do the Daniel fast (skip a meal; or give up certain foods and drinks for a 7 days).

Fasting

Where can you fast?

There really isn't any particular place *where* you should fast (not according to my knowledge of the Bible). Fasting is connected to prayer; therefore, I feel it can be done at home, job, school, church, etc.)

Why should you fast?

Fasting is a choice and to be done at your own discretion. **Some** reasons, you should fast (and pray), are as follows:

- Ministry (Acts 14:21-28)
- Worship: (Luke 2:36-38)
- Draw closer to HIM (James 4:8)
- Grief (Nehemiah 1:1-4)
- Repentance (Joel 2:12; Daniel 9:3-5)
- Humility (Psalms 35:13; Psalms 69:10; Ezra 8:21)
- Sickness (2 Samuel 12:15-17)
- Safe travels/protection (Ezra 8:21-23)

Fasting

How should you fast?

Fasting should be done privately; in secret. It should be a joyful experience.

When you fast, do not look somber as the hypocrites do, for they disfigure their faces to show others they are fasting. Truly I tell you, they have received their reward in full (**Matthew 6:16**).

But when you fast, put anointing oil (olive oil- **1Samuel 10:1; Exodus 29:7**) on your head and wash your face, so that it will not be obvious to others that you are fasting, but only to your Father, who is unseen; and your Father, who sees what is done in secret, will reward you openly (**Matthew 6:16-18**).

My prayer today is

Chapter 5

**God Is Calling
US
to
Use Our Senses
to
Spread His Word**

use our senses

God created humans in HIS image (**Genesis 1:26**). When God created us (**Genesis 1:27**), He gave us five (5) senses plus one extra and HE is calling us to use them spiritually (not just naturally). The 5 senses are:

SEE

We know God is a spirit and we cannot physically see Him (**Exodus 33:20; 1 Timothy 6:15-16**). God wants us to witness His power. There are multiple times His glory and power was shown throughout the Bible:

"Then the Lord said, *"Behold, there is a place by Me, and you shall stand there on the rock; and it will come about, while My glory is passing by, that I will put you in the cleft of the rock and cover you with My hand until I have passed by. Then I will take My hand away and you shall see My back, but My face shall not be seen* (**Exodus 33:21-23**)."

use our senses

"*Then the Lord came down in a pillar of cloud and stood at the doorway of the tent, and He called Aaron and Miriam. When they had both come forward, He said, "Hear now My words: (Numbers 12:5-6).*"

"*But being full of the Holy Spirit, Stephen gazed intently into heaven and saw the glory of God, and Jesus standing at the right hand of God; and he said, "Behold, I see the heavens opened up and the Son of Man standing at the right hand of God (Acts 7:55-56).*"

These are just a few examples of various ones witnessing the "glory and power" of God. Whatever the situation, we've all had a "but God" experience. At some point in our life, we have seen God's power. Maybe healed from a terrible disease or sickness; shielded from a horrible accident; escaping the brink of death; getting a major promotion or job with or without a degree; or unable to have children.

use our senses

Let's not be "doubting Thomases." We don't have to physically see God to know He exist. Those who don't tempt the Lord (about seeing Him with their natural eyes) are more blessed than "doubters" or nonbelievers (John 20:24-29). Receive Christ today and see the beauty of the Lord in all His glory (Psalms 27:4).

Hear

How many times have you heard that "still small voice (1King 19:11-13)." in the back of your mind letting you know that you are making the wrong decision? Did you take heed or obey? or Did you ignore it?

What happens when we take heed to or obey God's voice? Here a few scriptures to remind us: *"Has the Lord as much delight in burnt offerings and sacrifices as in obeying the voice of the Lord?*

use our senses

*Behold, to obey is better than sacrifice, and to heed than the fat of rams (**1 Samuel 15:22**)."*

*"according to the foreknowledge of God the Father, by the sanctifying work of the Spirit, to obey Jesus Christ and be sprinkled with His blood: May grace and peace be yours in the fullest measure (**1 Peter 1:2**)."*

*But He said, "On the contrary, blessed are those who hear the word of God and observe it (**Luke 11:28**)."*
*"But one who looks intently at the perfect law, the law of liberty, and abides by it, not having become a forgetful hearer but an effectual doer, this man/woman will be blessed in what he/she does (**James 1:25**)."*

Upon reading the aforementioned scriptures, I hope you have a better understanding as to why you should "listen out" for the voice of God and obey it.

Here are a few scriptures to explain what happens when we "refuse" to hear God's voice:

use our senses

- *"To whom shall I speak and give warning that they may hear? Behold, their ears are closed and they cannot listen. Behold, the word o f the Lord has become a reproach to them; they have no delight in it (Jeremiah 6:10)".*
- *"For this is a rebellious people, false sons; Sons who refuse to listen to the instruction of the Lord; (Isaiah 30:9)."*
- *"Concerning him we have much to say, and it is hard to explain, since you have become dull of hearing (Hebrews 5:11)."*

- *"For the heart of this people is waxed gross, and their ears are dull of hearing, and their eyes have they closed; lest they should see with their eyes, and hear with their ears, and understand with their heart, and should be converted, and I should heal them (Acts 28:27; Matthew 13:15)."*

Can you see the importance of listening to hear God's voice?

use our senses

Savor the flavor! As babes in Christ, we start out with "spiritual milk" (**1 Peter 2:2; Hebrews 5:12-13; 1 Corinthians 3:1-3**). We are learning what conversion is from sinner to saint. No one can tell you how long your infant-to-adolescent stage in Christ will be or should be. Let every man/woman run this race with patience and endurance (**Hebrews 12:1**).

When you are mature enough in Christ, then you will be able to eat "spiritual meat" (**Hebrews 5:14**). When you have tasted the good Word of God (**Hebrews 6:1-5**), God will let you know when it is time for you to move forward in Him.

Now saints and friends we know that "gluttony" which is overindulging in non- and alcoholic beverages or food (Deuteronomy 21:20; Proverbs 23:21) is a sin. Seriously. Anyone can love too much of anything or someone. To the point that he/she no longer puts God first or even think on Him before catering to the flesh. This is a sin because our bodies are the temple of Christ (1 Corinthians 3:16).

use our senses

We have to be careful not only what we put on it, but also, what we put in it. In order to be servants of Christ, we need to be sober and vigilant (**1 Peter 5:8**). Overindulging in food and drinks can make us tired and lazy which leads to "slothfulness" physically and spiritually (**Ecclesiastes 10:18; Proverbs 10:4-5; 12:24; 26:13-16**).

In my opinion, gluttony:

- causes *alcoholism* (too much alcoholic beverages on a daily basis),
- causes *obesity* (eating constantly without self-control),
- implies **lack of self-control** (ability to control one's behavior, emotions, and/or desires),
- promotes **greediness** (excess desire for food and/or drink, money, etc.), and
- signifies **idolatry** (love anything/anyone more than God).

Figure 1

use our senses

I am not writing this to persuade anyone not to eat or drink excessively; however, I am merely trying to bring ones attention to "taste/eat/drink" more healthily with smaller portions and in moderation. The physical body needs the proper nourishment and nutrients in order to function properly.

Remember, digestion is a process (see figure 1). The same goes without saying for spiritual food (**Matthew 4:4**) and drink (**1 Peter 2:2**). Even spiritually, one needs to eat/drink in small portions and in moderation so as not to burn out too quickly in serving God.

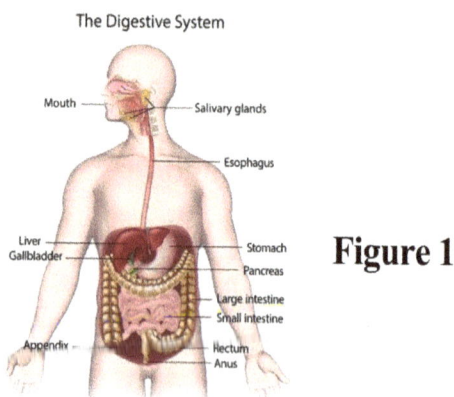

Figure 1

Remember, there is a process for spiritual development (*see figure 2*).

use our senses

Figure 2

Again, pray about it. The scripture says "let every man be persuaded by his/her own mind (**Romans 14:5**). You should not be judged by anyone either way.

use our senses

"Oh taste and see that the Lord is good (**Psalms 34:8**)!" God wants us to be "good gluttons"; not for earthly food but spiritual hunger for the Word of God. Eat the Word daily for it is healthy to your soul. Whoever feasts on the Word of God will never die; but have eternal life (**John 6:26-27, 58;**). God's word is bitter sweet:

"So I went to the angel and asked him to give me the little scroll. He said to me, "Take it and eat it. It will turn your stomach sour, but 'in your mouth it will be as sweet as honey. I took the little scroll from the angel's hand and ate it. It tasted as sweet as honey in my mouth, but when I had eaten it, my stomach turned sour" (**Revelation 10:9-10**).

"How sweet are Your words to my taste! Yes, sweeter than honey to my mouth!" (**Psalms 119:103**). Will you "taste" God's Word today?

use our senses

Touch

Hot; cold; pressure; pain. These are related to the sense of touch. When you think of a "touch" from God, which is the first thing comes to mind?:

Healing;
"*And all the people were trying to touch Him, for power was coming from Him and healing them all.*"

~Luke 6:19

"*Wherever He entered villages, or cities, or countryside, they were laying the sick in the market places, and imploring Him that they might just touch the hem of His cloak; and as many as touched it were being cured.*"

~Mark 6:56

Salvation/Repentance

"*Behold, the LORD's hand is not shortened, that it cannot save;*" ~Isaiah 59:1

use our senses

- **Conviction**

    "And when he comes, he will convict the world concerning sin and righteousness and judgment:"
    ~John 16:8

    "All Scripture is breathed out by God and profitable for
    teaching, for reproof, for correction, and for training in righteousness,"
    ~2 Timothy 3:16

    I remember my first touch from the Lord...**hot**! It was when I received him into my life. Oh what a wonderful feeling! Like the rays of warm sunshine bursting through an icy, cold window! HIS Holy Spirit touched my heart; filled it with joy, love, and peace. Such a high (a great adrenaline rush)!

    Another touch I received from God was not so pleasant (but beneficial and needful)--**cold; pressure; pain**! It was when I was "chastened/disciplined" by HIM (**Hebrews 12:6-7**). I called myself throwing a tantrum against the Lord; refusing to pray and seek HIM because I was in my feelings.

use our senses

I was upset with HIM. It seemed like I prayed and prayed but, my prayer went unanswered. I was left grief-stricken, confused, shocked, and angry.

"Pray!" HE says. "Why should I?" I say. This went on for quite a while. When God saw enough was enough, He "pricked" my heart...convicted me! Of course, not physically "prick" my heart! But definitely, spiritually! God reminded me that HE is in control and all things work together for my good (Romans 8:28; Isaiah 45:6-7).

Praise Jesus for HIS mercy, grace, and compassion rather than touching me out of anger during my tantrum! I mean, who wants to fall into the hands of an angry God (Hebrews 10:31; Ezra 8:22); not me!

Have you ever been touched by God? If so, how did it make you feel?

use our senses

🗢 Smell 🗢

Imagine each scenario:

1. *You have had such a hard day at work. You get home. Turn the key and open the door. There is a pleasant aroma coming from the kitchen! It's your favorite meal being prepared. You sit down and relax. Eyes blissful! Sniffing that delightful odor! Licking your lips, smacking your teeth, and rubbing your belly! Satisfying!*
2. *You have had such a hard day at work. You get home. Walking up the steps. Your face stiffens. Angry eyes. Nose turned up. Skunky smell. Stenchy odor! Ugh! You want to vomit! It's sewage! You sit down on the step and think to yourself: "I should have got this plumbing fixed last week instead of procrastinating!" Regretful.*

use our senses

Which odor or aroma concerning *me* relates to the nostrils of God? **Pleasant!** OR **Stinky!** Am I pleasing in HIS sight as a disciple of Christ (**Philippians 4:18**)? OR Do I make HIM so sick that HE wants to spew me out of HIS mouth (**Revelation 3:16**)?

God created humans in HIS image (**Genesis 1:27**). At one point in time, humans were so wicked and corrupt that God regretted creating them (**Genesis 6:6**). So He destroyed the entire earth with a flood (**Genesis 6:17**).

When the people of Sodom and Gomorrah were disobedient to God's will, it displeased Him. Their sins and corrupt ways polluted the air. The stench reached God's nostrils; so, HE destroyed Sodom and Gomorrah (**Genesis 19:13**). I feel that my soul is unpleasant (stinks) to God when I am out of HIS will and not committed to HIS ways.

use our senses

God loves the sweet smelling aroma of our sacrificial, fragrant offerings towards HIM (**Ephesians 5:2**)! After HE destroyed the earth with water the first time, Noah's burnt offerings was a "smell of sweet savor" to the Lord (**Genesis 8:21**). As we repent and accept Christ in our lives, HE will "accept us with our sweet savor."
(**2 Corinthians 2:15; Ezekiel 20:41**).

Offer up sacrifices of joy and praise today! Get to know the Savior. When I do what pleases God, I feel it gives off a sweet aroma!

Sixth Sense?
Discernment

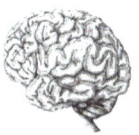
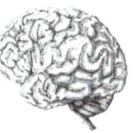

"Listen to that 'gut feeling'!" OR "If it's too good to be true, then it usually is!" Have you ever had anyone say this to you before? I have; several times. Including the Lord. I ignored it. It cost me in the long run! Figuratively and literally!

What is discernment or intuition? Do I have a ***"sixth sense"***?

- **Discernment**-having the ability to judge (with spiritual guidance and understanding).
- **Intuition**-having an "instinct" without conscious reasoning

Go to this website and take the quiz to see for yourself: https://www.proprofs.com/quiz-school/story.php? title=do-you-have-a-sixth-sense

use our senses

Discernment is akin to 'wisdom.' Discernment helps us **not** to be deceived by the devil and false prophets. It helps us to determine good from evil. (**1 Kings 3:9, 11; 1 John 4:1; Hebrews 5:14**).

When you have that "gut feeling" that something isn't quite right, please don't ignore it. God is sending you "red flags"-discernment/intuition. This could be in a personal relationship, attending a church service, or accepting a job. Pray to God about your 'sixth sense' (**Psalms 119:66, 125; Philippians 1:9-10**). We all have one (6th sense).

use our senses

Does it make sense to trust in idols? Use Your Senses

Psalms 115:4-11

4 Their idols are silver and gold, the work of men's hands.
5 They have mouths, but they speak not: eyes have they, but they see not:
6 They have ears, but they hear not: noses have they, but they smell not:
7 They have hands, but they handle not: feet have they, but they walk not: neither speak they through their throat.
8 They that make them are like unto them; so is every one that trusteth in them.
9 O Israel, trust thou in the Lord: he is their help and their shield.
10 O house of Aaron, trust in the Lord: he is their help and their shield.
11 Ye that fear the Lord, trust in the Lord: he is their help and their shield.

Spread The Word

Who hasn't spread lies, rumors or gossip before? If we answer truthfully, we are all guilty. "Rumors" and "lies" are close kin in meaning. A rumor is neither true nor untrue and travels quickly. A lie is totally false and told by someone to someone and travels quickly. Whether a rumor or lie, some of us feel untruths are more tantalizing or appealing than truths. We would rather believe the lie than the truth (**2 Thessalonians 2:11-12**).

God warns us that the devil is the father of all lies and untruths (**John 8:44**). He also tells us that every liar will have their part in the lake of fire (**Revelation 21:8**) and that a lying tongue is an abomination (**Proverbs 12:22**).

Instead of spreading rumors, lies, and gossip, let's spread God's Word. By doing so, we hope to either help others:

- gain knowledge of Christ (**Philippians 3:8; Jeremiah 3:15**);

Spread The Word

- seek Him for repentance (**Mark 16:16**); and/or
- become disciples of Christ as well (**Matthew 28:19**). "In the beginning was the Word, and the Word was with God, and the Word was God (**John 1:1**).

"To "spread the Word" is telling others about God, His Son- Jesus, and the Holy Spirit. Sharing your faith with others, attending Bible study, or volunteering in the community are a few ways you can get God's message out to others. Additionally, you can use social media and other online platforms to share scriptures and inspirational messages to a broader audience.

Spread The Word

In these perilous, alarming times we are living in (**2 Timothy 3:1-7**), God is calling us to spread the "gospel" of Jesus Christ (**Mark 16:15**). HE wants us to be ready "in season and out of season" (**2 Timothy 4:2**).

Many Christians feel it is solely the duty of the pastors and preachers to spread the Word. However; when we come into the knowledge of Christ and are saved from sinners to saints, we are equipped to minister the Word of God to others (**Ephesians 4:11-13; 2 Corinthians 3:6; Revelation 1:5-6**).

As we spread God's word, we really should use our senses.

My prayer today is

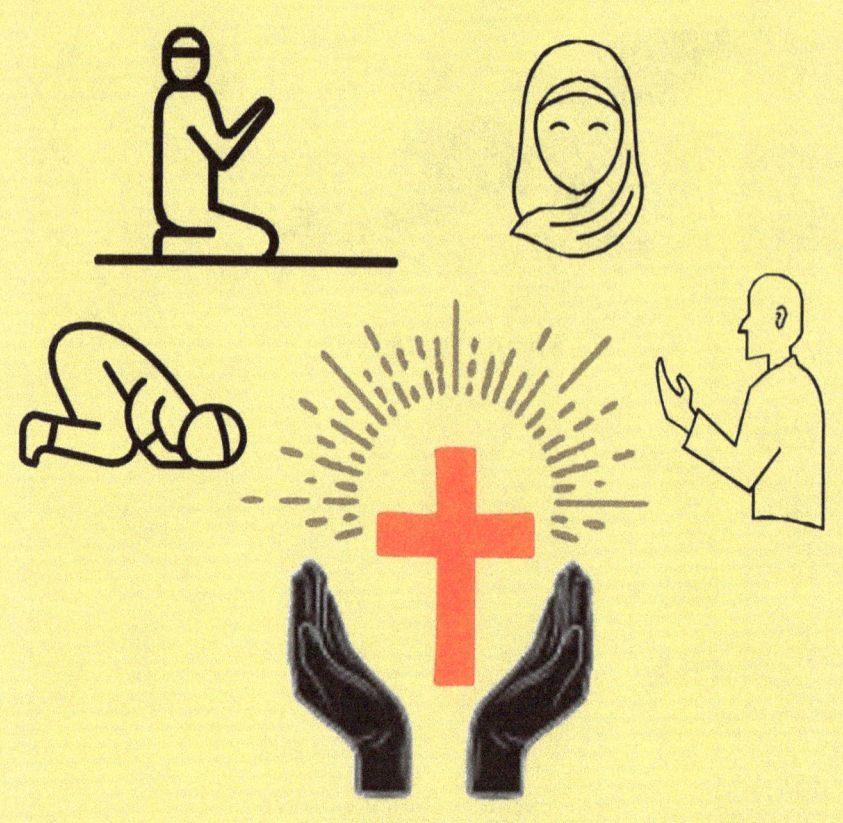

Chapter 6

**God is Calling
For
People to
Earnestly Forgive**

FORGIVENESS

If "forgiveness" was a pill prescribed by a doctor, it would be certainly hard to swallow. You could probably barely get it down your throat. Regardless of how much water you drank. Why is it so difficult to do? Forgive others? Forgive yourself?

It's easy to quote scripture: *"If you don't forgive those who trespass against you, then our Heavenly Father will not forgive your trespasses"* (**Matthew 6:15**). It's not enough to say you forgive someone. I mean, *"actions speak louder than words."*

Could it be that it's hard to forgive others because of pride, hatred, anger, or ego? Is it possible that resentment, guilt, shame, or regret causes people to withhold forgiveness from themselves? It doesn't matter how many times someone trespasses against you, you must still forgive them. How many times?

Jesus answered, "I tell you, not seven times, but until seventy times seven."(**Matthew 18:22~KJV**).

FORGIVENESS

It just doesn't seem fair. It seems as though the trespasser is getting away with hurting you; mistreating you; abusing you. You want revenge; to take matters in your own hands! *"We want justice! When do we want it? NOW!"* God seems to be moving too slow. One day HE let me know that "It is not your place to make another person reap! (**Galatians 6:7**). HE forgives everyone regardless of what they have done or is doing wrong. The wrongdoer will reap on God's terms and in HIS set time. But wait!! "Do not gloat when your enemy falls; when they stumble, do not let your heart rejoice, or the Lord will see and disapprove and turn HIS wrath away from them (**Proverbs 24:17- 18**). God has no respect of persons (**Romans 2:11**). You have to forgive from the heart; not just with the mouth. **How?** Seek God for understanding about how to forgive. Although we are mere humans, we must separate flesh from the Spirit. This may take some time and strong faith. Forgiving others is expected of every Christian and believer of Christ (**Matthew 5:8-39**). It seems easier said than done; however, it's not impossible. Think of how refreshing and wonderful you will feel afterwards!

FORGIVENESS

Forgiveness brings peace and joy to your soul! I know from experience. Let that wound scab over; stop picking at it. If you continue to do so (pick at that wound), it will never heal and may become infected. Forgive others! (Ephesians 4:32).

And now forgive yourself. Ask God to close the door on your past; your pain and then open the door to your new journey; your new beginning (**Philippians 4:8**). Forgive yourself!

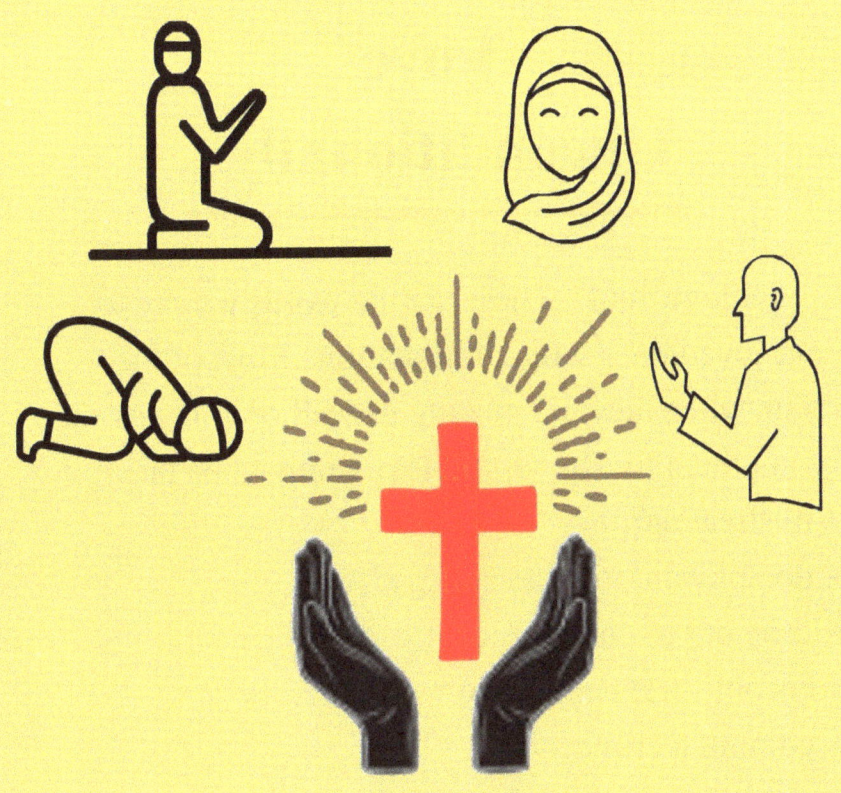

Chapter 7

**God Is Calling
For
People to
Love Unconditionally**

Love Unconditionally

"I love you!" These are the words we say to our loved ones without hesitation. Most of the time when they are treating us well or doing as we want them to. Do we **still love them** when they:
- mistreat us?, or
- do not want to go to college?, or
- drop out of college?, or
- become pregnant out of wedlock?,
- commit a crime?, or
- alcohol/substance abuse?, or
- LGBTQ?

The answer to the aforementioned questions should be "**YES!**" God does love us regardless (**1 John 4:7-8; 1 Peter 4:8**). HE has no respect of persons (**Romans 2:11**).

> Love bears all things, believes all things, hopes all things, endures all things. Love never ends.
> – 1 Corinthians 13:7

Love Unconditionally

As my children were getting older, it seemed as though I was loving them **on condition** instead of **unconditionally**. I didn't know how to handle parenting teenagers; especially as a single mom. I felt I was losing control over rearing them. I remember telling God, "Lord I don't understand this level of parenting and I'm so stressed." I remember God telling me that I have to "let go" and stop talking to them as if they are still babies. It's' okay to let them make mistakes. Continue to pray for them. You have taught them about "*ME*" (**Proverbs 22:6**).

Now that my son and daughter are young adults, we are the best of friends and talk to each other about **every**thing! I love them each unconditionally!

It is important for us to remember that we are an imperfect people. If the ones we trust and love do not live up to our standards or potential, we must love them still and treat them right (**Luke 6:27-28**).

Loving someone unconditionally does not mean nor require you to stay in a hostile environment or toxic/abusive relationship. God has called us to live in peace (**Romans 5:1-2; 1 Corinthians 7:15**).

Love Unconditionally

Unconditional Love:
no conditions to loving another;
no expectations to do anything to make either person feel loved; each person is loved for being themself;
selfless

Conditional Love:
need expectations to make each other feel loved and accepted;
seeks control;
looks to be completed and validated by another person;
selfish

Today, are you loving someone 'on condition' or 'unconditionally'?

My prayer today is

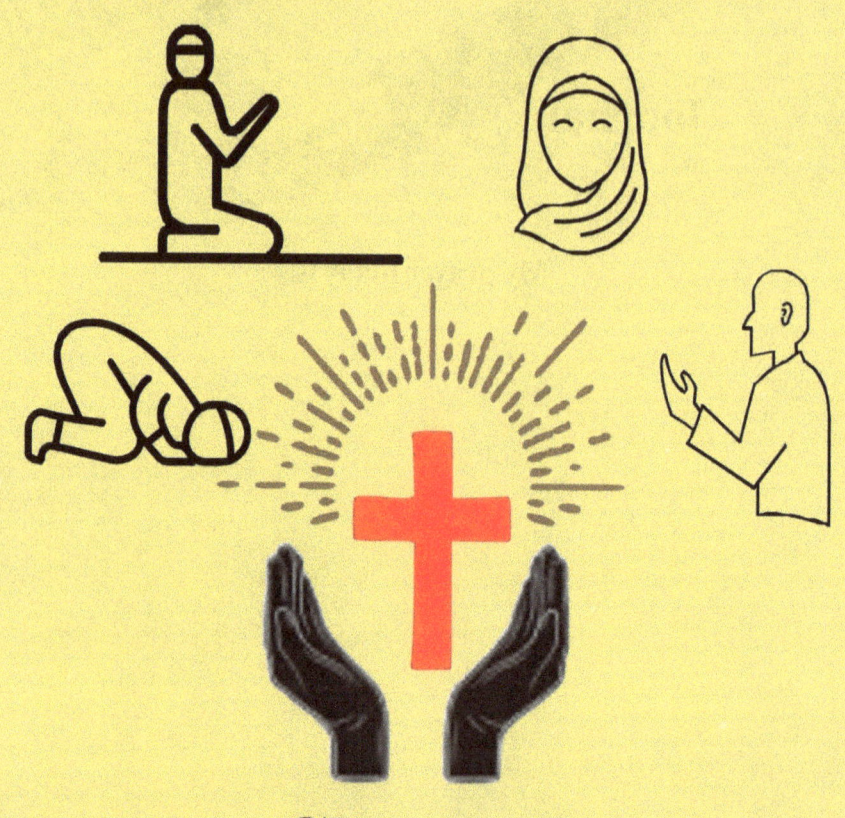

Chapter 8

**God Is Calling
For
Victors of the Spirit vs. Victims of the
Flesh**

Spirit vs. Flesh

At some point in your life , you have experienced that "right or wrong" voice. Some say it's that angel on one side and the devil whispering to you on the other. Spirit versus the flesh (**2 Corinthians 10:3**).

Your spirit wants to do what is right; however, the flesh is weak causing you to make an immoral decision (**Matthew 26:41**). Like a kid getting their hand caught in the cookie jar!

What is the "spirit" of humans? It is your inner being; the inner man; the soul; the Godly heart of mankind (Ephesians 3:16; Galatians 5:16). And the flesh? The outer man or outer being; the human body (Galatians 5:19-21) and its members (1 Corinthians 12:12).

Spirit vs. Flesh

What is the "spirit" of humans? It is your inner being; the inner man; the soul; the Godly heart of mankind (**Ephesians 3:16; Galatians 5:16**). And the flesh? The outer man or outer being; the human body (**Galatians 5:19-21**) and its members (**1 Corinthians 12:12**).

The spirit and the flesh are always at war with each other (**Galatians 5:17**). For example, read these two (2) scenarios below:

1. John Doe is in the 8th grade and needs to pass his final Math exam. He has his notes on a post-it and questions within himself whether to use it while taking the exam. "What if I get caught?!," he thinks. "I know better than cheating." he says to himself. He pulled out the post-it and stared at it. He felt so nervous, anxious, and ashamed. He balled up the paper and threw it away, took the exam, and passed! "Thank God!" he said to himself.

Spirit vs. Flesh

2. There was a beautiful, young woman who is married for numerous years; yet unhappy in her marriage. She met a handsome young man while shopping one day, and they talked with each other. He asked her to meet him for dinner. Immediately she thought, "What's the harm; it's just dinner?" After a couple of more dinner dates, he told her to meet him at a hotel. She contemplated and thought, "What if I get caught?!" She told him she will think about it and give him a call later. Two days passed and she called him. They met. "I know better than cheating?!", she told herself. "But I'm unhappy with   , and this guy makes me happy," she thought. Desires were fulfilled. She debated with herself and said, "I think I will see him again. I know it's wrong, but I can't help myself!"

Who gave in to the spirit? Who obeyed the flesh?

Spirit vs. Flesh

Reminder: The spirit and the flesh are always warring against each other. The spirit does what is right while the flesh succumbs to fleshly desires (**Romans 13:14; Galatians 5:16**). How can my spirit override my flesh when my flesh is so weak?

Repentance (Godly sorrow for ones sins) is the key to fulfilling the spirit and denying the lusts of the flesh (**Romans 6:6; 13:14; Mark 8:34;**). Once we become knowledgeable about Christ and surrender to HIM, we should no longer satisfy nor cater to the desires of the flesh (**Galatians 5:24; Romans 8:1-2**). Jesus Christ will give us a new heart, mind, and the Holy Spirit (**Ezekiel 36:26-27; Psalms 51:10; Romans 12:2**).

Spirit vs. Flesh

Temptation

Is your flesh weak today? Seek God in prayer. Do **not** enter into temptation!

Attempt versus tempt. **"Attempt"** means to try. **"Tempt"** means provoking or rightfully/wrongfully enticing someone with the means to receive a reward or promise. So when we attempt to tempt someone, we are trying to get something in return by attracting them to their desires.

The devil (the tempter) made several attempts to tempt Jesus after the fast in the wilderness (Matthew 4:1-11). We are not better than Jesus Christ; which is why we are tempted by the tempter (devil) continually. It is not the Lord who tempts us, but the devil (James 1:13-16).

Temptation comes when we are weak and seeking after the cares of the world and our fleshly desires-- lust of the flesh, lust of the eyes, and the pride of life (1 John 2:16). To give in to temptation one is carnally minded-- fulfilling the lust of the flesh (Romans 8:5).

Spirit vs. Flesh

Temptation

There are many ways we are tempted. Some are:
- sexually (strip clubs; pornography, ,fornication, adultery, etc.),
- materialistically (lover of money, idolatry, impulsive shopping, etc.),
- psychologically (slothfulness, procrastination, lying, fearfulness, etc.), and/or
- socially (gossiping, showing partiality (favoritism), bullying, cyberbullying, etc.)

It is important to remember that God provides an escape route for temptation, and we are not tempted above that we are able (**1 Corinthians 10:13**). This is why we must watch and pray that we do not get trapped by temptation (**Matthew 26:41**); neither give place to the devil (**Ephesians 4:27**). For we are not ignorant of the devil's devices (**2 Corinthians 2:11**). We will receive a crown of life if we endure temptation. This is a promise from God (**James 1:12-16**).

Are you being tempted by the devil today? Please submit yourself to God; resist the devil; and the devil will flee (**James 4:7**).

My prayer today is

Chapter 9

**God is Calling
For
People to
Use Spiritual Gift(s)
and/or
Natural Talent(s)**

Gifts and Talents

Everyone has a natural talent and/or spiritual gift. Some one; some few; others many. Maybe you just haven't tapped into it or discovered it yet. Or maybe you are afraid.

Talents and gifts are often confused with one another. Talents are naturally or genetically received from birth or well-learned skills achieved later in life (e.g., music, singing, athletics, carpentry, artistry, etc.).

Spiritual gifts are given by God and HIM alone! Spiritual gift(s) like healing, prophesy, wisdom, speaking in tongues, interpreting unknown tongues, teachers, preachers, etc. come after you accept Christ in your life. Some may argue this point, but I base it on scriptures (**1 Corinthians 12:1-31; Ephesians 4:11-13; Romans 12:1-21; 1 Timothy 4:14; Galatians 5:22-23**) of my understanding.

Gifts and Talents

Some people say, "I don't have a talent nor a gift." Trust me, you have a talent (if you just search within yourself). Have you ever heard you need to "find your niche?" A niche (pronounced neesh or nitch) is similar to "a calling" or "a vocation." This is kind of how you discover your talent. You have to figure out something you do very well at and hone in on it. Focus. Educate yourself. Work at it. Perfect it.

For example, you may have a passion to sew (without even cutting out a pattern). Keep practicing hard enough until you perfect it. Before you know it, you will be an entrepreneur; providing a service to the community and abroad.

Don't be afraid to broaden your horizons. It's okay to do things out of your comfort zone. Hidden talent(s) is/are found in each of us. We have to discover it. Maybe use it or lose it. Remember the parable of the talents in the Bible (**Matthew 25:14-30**)?

Gifts and Talents

Gift(s) or talent(s). No need to envy others. You have one or many as well. Search within yourself for your talent(s) and seek God for your spiritual gift(s) which will manifest itself once you accept Christ. Don't be afraid of how old or young you are; of how much time has passed you by; or of how many have already discovered theirs. Ask God to remove doubt and fear (**2 Timothy 1:7**).

My prayer today is

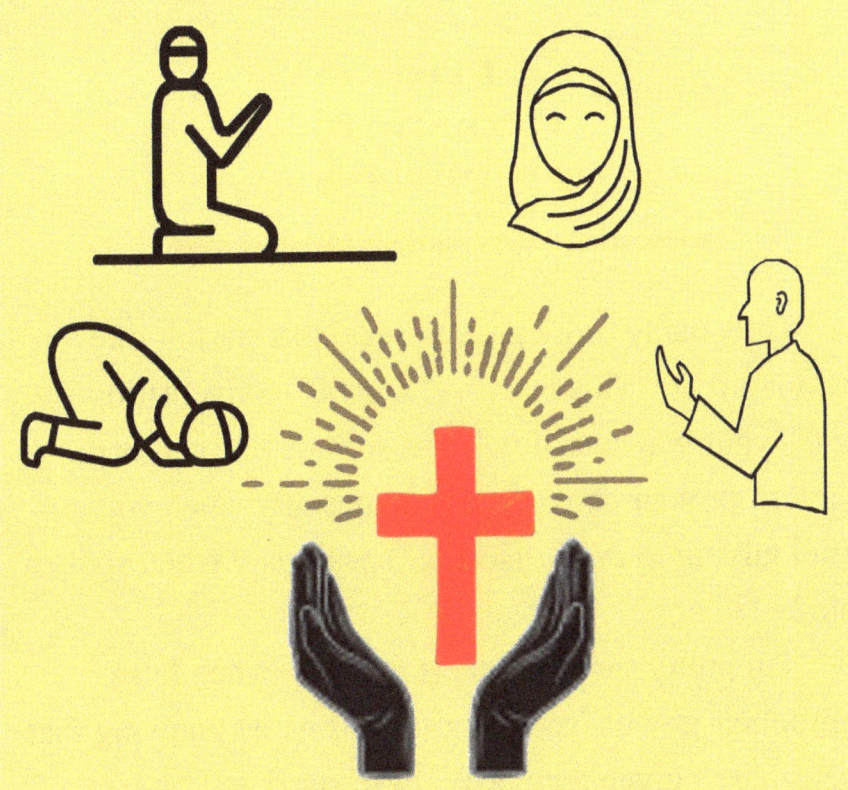

Chapter 10

**God Is Calling
For A
True Prophet/Prophetess**

True Prophet/prophetess

How many times have we said this (or felt like saying it)?: "This is an "A" and "B" conversation; so, "C" your way out of it." It is so rude for people to interrupt your conversation; especially when you are not talking to them. Hence, "speak only when spoken to."

I'm pretty sure God feels this way when false prophets go out "speaking" in His name knowing that HE hasn't given them a Word to speak to you (**Jeremiah 14:14**). One of their (false prophets/prophetess) infamous sayings is: "God told me to tell you _____."

How do I or you know he/she is a false prophet/prophetess? Well, the Word (which is God) will come to you first and tell you what HE (God) wants you to know and do.

True Prophet/prophetess

HE uses the prophet/prophetess for confirmation. That prophetic Word will come to pass (if God sent them to you) **Deuteronomy 13:1-5; 18:20-22**.

One example is when God commanded Elijah, the Tishbite, to go to Zarephath to receive a meal from the widow woman and her son, HE (God) had already spoken to the widow woman first. The scripture says "Arise...I have commanded a widow woman there to sustain thee (**1 Kings 17:9**)." When Elijah arrived, the widow woman did as God already instructed her to do so.

When we accept Jesus Christ as our Lord and Savior, He opens up our knowledge and understanding of Him. God the Father, God the Son, and the Holy Spirit are One (**1 Peter 1:2**). HE will speak to you and a stranger's voice you will not hear (John 10:-5); unless you have "itching ears" (**2 Timothy 4:3**) to hear only what you want to hear.

True Prophet/prophetess

God is calling us to speak only when spoken to and what HE speaks to you; especially if you have the gift of prophecy (**Romans 12:6; Acts 2:16-17**). We must rely on and trust the Holy Spirit to lead us so as not to satisfy the deeds of the flesh, (**Galatians 5:16; John 16:13; 2 Peter 1:21**) say what we want to say to get others to listen, and/or for our personal gain (e.g., control, money, power, etc.).

"Although you're not doing the best you can, at least you're doing better than you were."
~Ruth Hampton~

2013 Graduate of UNC-Charlotte-
M.Ed. in Special Education-General Curriculum-K-12

ABOUT RUTH HAMPTON

I am a mother, grandmother, daughter, sister, auntie, and former educator who loves to write inspirational literature (based upon my Christian faith). I enjoy sharing my spiritual knowledge and wisdom of Christ with others; hoping they will accept Him as their Savior some day.

When she is not writing, Ishe enjoys spending time with family, travelling, cooking, sewing, arts and crafts, and working as an educator. She is a firm believer that salvation and education are fundamental keys to living a successful life!

www.ingramcontent.com/pod-product-compliance
Lightning Source LLC
Chambersburg PA
CBHW071121160426
43196CB00013B/2660